Mended Nuptials

Other Books
by Dr. Gary L. Williams Sr.:

Man to Man
Why Can't I Hold On to This Grudge?
Deliverance from the Down Low
Family Drama
Prevailing over Pornography
21 Days to Breakthrough

Mended Nuptials

It's Going to Cost You

Dr. Gary L. Williams Sr.

So He Writes, LLC
Jacksonville, FL

ISBN: 978-1-7342602-0-5 - Paperback
eISBN: 978-1-7342602-1-2 - ePub
eISBN: 978-1-7342602-2-9 - mobi

Library of Congress Control Number: 2020903385

Printed in the United States of America   0 3 2 7 2 0

⊗This paper meets the requirements of ANSI/NISO Z39.48-1992 (Permanence of Paper)

This book is dedicated to every couple who authentically desires to protect, preserve, and restore the institution of what God has joined together.

*So they are no longer two but one flesh. What therefore
God has joined together, let not man separate.*
—Matthew 19:6, ESV

Contents

Introduction

Most people are familiar with nuptials which state, "Until death do us part." It refers to the ideas that physical death will be the only thing that should sever a marriage. Recent times have brought a different meaning to the phrase.

Presently, it is not physical death but rather a myriad of other things that has led to a backlog of divorce cases. From irreconcilable differences to plain old dishonesty, the seams of many marriages are coming apart no sooner than people are brought together. More than ever before, the word love has been tossed around like a frisbee. Like a disposable razor after being used a dozen times, the sharpness is lost. The same holds true for many marriages. After the wedding, honeymoon, mind-blowing sex, kids, a new vehicle, and a house, the thrill is soon gone. The ground that was once firm is slowly transformed into quicksand. The vows recited with warmth and genuineness in front of friends and family becomes a thing of the past.

A major contributing factor to failed nuptials is the assumption that love will solve all problems. This thought process is Pollyanna, to say the least. Love does not solve problems; solutions do. Love is unconditional; however, there are conditions and requirements that make a marriage successful. While love is a major reason for bringing people together, working to resolve relational differences in addition to love is what keeps people together.

Several years ago while experiencing equilibrium problems, I made an appointment to see my ENT doctor.

After my initial visit, they ordered a caloric test. This is a test designed to see if there is an imbalance or a problem with the sensory system. The sensory system is what provides the body with spatial orientation and contributes to your sense of balance. This deals with hand, eye, and brain coordination as well as depth perception. The caloric test was designed to either pinpoint the problem or eliminate what was not the problem. I was instructed to lie back in a chair while the technician ran cold and hot water in my ears. The intention was to cause the room to spin—and spin it did. To get the room to stop spinning, the technician said, "When I sit you up, find a ceiling tile to focus on and don't take your eyes off of it. Doing this will make the room stop spinning much faster as opposed to gazing all over the room."

Those who truly desire to stop their marriage from spinning, it is essential that they are not gazing at things that are not the problem. However, focus collectively on solving the problems, because your problems will not solve themselves.

Chapter One
Let's Take It from the Top

The reasons for committing adultery can be as numerous as the rocks in the Grand Canyon. Good marriages often end up on the rocks because someone was searching for greener pastures. Despite how strong or spiritual a marriage is or may appear to be, no marriage is exempt from being shattered by adultery. Regardless of why, how, or when the infidelity occurred, the roots of infidelity usually begin the same way.

Infidelity occurs because of a lack of respect. No matter how you examine it, disregard and the lack of respect are always at ground zero of adultery. A disregard for vows, feelings, attention, and self-worth are just a few of the culprits responsible for sending a marriage off the cliff. In a marriage that has been rocky from the start, adultery is often expected. However, when a marriage has been steady but still goes astray, adultery seems surreal.

Despite the difficulties that confront a marriage, adultery is often the last thing imagined by the faithful spouse. Adultery opens a wide range of feelings and emotions that probably have been foreign to the relationship. Rage, anger, retaliation, pain, regret, and deception are just a few of the emotions that one must temper to bring a sense of normalcy back to a world that adultery has turned upside down.

Many people are familiar with the colloquial phrase,

"You don't miss the water until the well runs dry." This definitely applies to fidelity in a marriage. It is important for couples to know that infidelity has been compared to, and often bears a resemblance to, death.

The spouse that experiences the impact of its brutality could well compare it to death. The weight of moving from feeling affection to not knowing what to feel or feeling nothing at all is a burden that most find unbearable. Amid the depth of the pain and the devastation of one's feelings, if both parties are open and willing to renew the commitment, then all is not lost.

Taking it from the top addresses the couple's ability to start all over again. Before we begin, it is essential that we establish the rules of engagement. The key to the restoration of marriage is based upon both parties having the same objective. Let me be clear, there is a difference between having a similar objective and the same objective. Frog legs might taste like chicken; however, they are not the same. Cleanliness may be likened to godliness; however, being clean will not make you godly.

Many years ago, while selling cars, I was taught an invaluable lesson that continues to resonate with me today. When I was selling Fords, my manager taught me that before overcoming an objective, the objective must first be defined. The difference between a top salesman and the typical salesman is the top salesman's ability to define and overcome goals. Exceptional salespeople identify and seek to overcome the obstacles pertaining to reaching their objective. Regardless of whether the roadblock was a payment, price, color, equipment, or spousal approval, the key to moving vehicles was to pinpoint the hindrance and sell vehicles.

ACKNOWLEDGE WHAT YOU DID

Acknowledgment must be confronted when addressing infidelity. Admitting the infidelity is at the epicenter of moving a relationship forward. It is important to understand what is meant by acknowledging the problem. Owning up to the problem is much more than simply being caught, apologizing, purchasing an "I'm sorry" gift, and attempting to move on.

Several years ago, a high-profile athlete was discovered to have had an extramarital affair. Once the affair was made public, the athlete went into serious damage-control mode. He apologized to his fans, team, and his wife. As a token of his remorse, he bought his wife a ring worth several million dollars. Just as the athlete's affair became public, the purchase of the ring and the reason for its purchase also became public knowledge.

Who would want to wear such a ring, one that everyone would know the reason behind its purchase? Can't you hear people saying, "Oh, what a gorgeous ring. Oh yeah, that was the ring your husband bought you after he was found to have been cheating on you." *Things* don't mend relationships; people do. It's not the superficial, but the spiritual things that bring a relationship back together.

FULL DISCLOSURE

Acknowledging the problem addresses several concerns: first, what happened, and second, when did it happen? In answering the first question, it is essential that there is full disclosure. Answering the "what" is the first step to a long stairwell of recovery. In baseball, a player cannot go to second base until he lawfully goes to first base. Scores of marriages fail in the attempt to recover from a serious setback because someone tries to circumvent the necessary bases. You are fooling yourself if you think you can move forward without touching first base.

When it comes to mending a marriage that has been damaged by infidelity, first base involves identifying exactly what happened. It is important for the culprit who is responsible for the infidelity not to compound the problem by claiming the Fifth Amendment or by playing ignorant.

Let me be perfectly clear, acknowledging the "what" means to lay all the cards out on the table. Laying all the cards on the table means making a full disclosure about all aspects of the involvement. As difficult as it may be, the guilty party must be willing to tell the entire truth about what occurred.

During my years of counseling, I have often come across a spouse who is not willing to make full disclosure. I have even had some tell me that they didn't think it was necessary to discuss the details. However, they want to continue counseling—without full disclosure. Can you imagine purchasing a puzzle with a few missing pieces? A puzzle can never be complete until all the pieces are in the right places. The same holds true when the vows of a marriage are fractured. Until all the pieces are in place, the marriage will remain an incomplete puzzle.

DISCLOSURE, DECEPTION, DETOUR

Many people are afraid to make full disclosure because they feel their spouse will vacate the marriage.

However, this is a consequence one must be willing to face after having made a full disclosure. It would be far better for their spouse to leave after having heard the full disclosure rather than to attempt to move forward in the relationship only to discover some new revelation. When a marriage is reeling because of deception, it is placed on extremely thin ice.

Deception may place your marriage in a coffin; however, compounded deception is the nail that will seal the coffin shut. The initial part of acknowledging infidelity addresses disclosure. The second aspect of acknowledgment addresses the detour.

Whereas disclosure addresses what happened in the marriage, the detour addresses when it happened. Let me emphasize that confronting the detour is in one way even more important than the disclosure. The detour brings insight into when the marriage began to go off track. The ability to spot the detour is important because it helps to thwart the marriage from going astray again. Keep in mind that relationships detour for various reasons.

The reasons for infidelity are as different as the east is from the west. Extramarital affairs are at an all-time high, and more of them are occurring because of an emotional void rather than sexual attraction. The lack of attention in a marriage is often the point of the wedge that drives a spouse into the arms or the bedroom of another. Many detours occur because one spouse was emotionally deprived. A lack of affection, attention, or attraction is the perfect mixture for infidelity.

Many relationships suffer because there was a detour pertaining to the intimacy in the marriage. Usually when a marriage lacks larger intimacies, it's because smaller intimacies were absent. When there are small signs of affection constantly taking place, larger intimacies will come naturally.

Small intimacies are the daily affections one spouse extends to the other. Small intimacies range from a brief kiss goodbye and an occasional "I love you," to holding hands in public or other acts of endearment. Small intimacies are the kind gestures that frequently and naturally take place in the matrimony. Moreover, they are intimacies that primarily take place outside of the bedroom.

When small intimacies are absent in a marriage, the marriage often seems more like a partnership than a marriage. Larger intimacies are intimacies that primarily take place in the bedroom. When there is boredom in the bedroom, it's usually because there's boredom in all the other rooms of the house.

Many relationships decline or detour because they have grown sterile. Before elaborating further, it is essential that we distinguish the difference between the relationship that was sidetracked and one that was never on track. The information I am sharing addresses a marriage that was sidetracked, not one that was never on track.

Relationships grow sterile because people do not finish what they started, or they attempt to be something that they are not. Either way is a recipe for disaster. Another detour is when you need family or friends in your midst to have a good time with each other. When a relationship grows sterile, it is impotent and cold. When you become cold to your spouse's feelings, hurts, insecurities, and desires, their fantasy begins to look better than the facts. Moreover, detours occur when one is taken for granted.

Those of us who have been driving for any length of time are familiar with road detours. Just as there are physical detour signs, there are marital detour signs. An example of a marital detour sign is a spouse's willingness to do, without hesitation, what someone outside of the marriage has asked him or her to do, but is always hesitant or slow to do what is asked of them inside the marriage. To keep a fractured marriage together, all attention must be focused on mending the fracture. Repairing the breach involves bringing the problem front and center and addressing it head on.

ADDRESSING
HURTS AND HINDRANCES

One cannot completely concentrate on disclosure and detours without tackling hurts and hindrances. The hindrance of the problem is the culprit. Anytime infidelity occurs, two culprits must be dealt with. The primary culprit is the cheating spouse, and the secondary culprit is the person he or she cheated with.

Many times, the spouse who is hurt often places their attention on the wrong culprit. The wrong culprit is the person outside the marriage. In fact, that culprit is only secondary, and has had only a cameo appearance in the affair. The primary culprit is the main character of the plot. Therefore, it becomes the responsibility of the primary culprit to amend his or her egregious act.

Serious problems call for serious solutions. It is the responsibility of the primary hindrance to abandon all ties with the secondary hindrance. This calls for drastic measures. If the same company employs both the transgressing spouse and the person with whom he or she has had the affair, saving the marriage will more than likely require a change of venue.

Tackling the hindrance involves changing phone numbers, email addresses, and severing all other forms of communication, including dialogue with the sinning party. A former state official was discovered to have been having an affair. For several days, he was mysteriously absent from his office. No one knew of his whereabouts—not his wife, his secretary, nor the state's officials.

The state official had gone to great lengths to mask his infidelity. He shared with certain members of his staff the untruth that he would be hiking in a place that he was not. Once the truth was exposed, it was discovered that he had traveled to another country to be with a woman he called his "soul mate." Upon returning home, the disgraced politician apologized; however, he did something that I highly recommend against. In mentioning the people that he had hurt, he spoke of hurting his mistress first, then his state, his boys, his wife, and his friends—in that order.

It is not my intent to be too critical, but the first person he should have apologized to was his wife. The state official was fully aware when he traveled abroad that he left a faithful wife and handsome boys at home. To further compound his attempt at an apology, he stated publicly that the mistress was his soul mate. There is no perfect way to end an extramarital relationship. However, when one attempts to culminate an extramarital relationship, his or her actions must be swift, decisive, firm, and complete.

FULL DISCLOSURE FROM THE NONCULPABLE SPOUSE

There should be no final dates, goodbye cruises, or one for the road; just end it! Mending a fractured relationship addresses the hurt as well as the hindrance. Part of addressing the hurt in the relationship involves getting rid of the hindrance. Just as the spouse who is the culprit of the infidelity must make a full and complete disclosure, the spouse who has been damaged needs to make a full disclosure as well.

Full disclosure on behalf of the damaged spouse must be made to clear the air. The innocent spouse must make a full disclosure for different reasons than the guilty spouse. It is imperative that the hurting spouse share his or her feelings, because failing to do so could very well lead to a false sense of progress in the marriage. As mentioned earlier, before you can overcome an objective, the objective must first be defined. Rome wasn't built in a day, and the damage to your marriage will not be repaired in a day.

The extent of that damage to the marriage must be disclosed and monitored if true progress is to be made toward mending the relationship. Disclosure of the injury does not mean it must be discussed every day. However, it must be addressed spiritually and professionally. I highly recommend that couples seek spiritual or professional counseling to help them through these difficult times. In many cases, the transgressing spouse will be the first to buck against seeking counseling. Regardless of how much he or she bucks, hold your ground and demand counseling.

Let me warn you in advance: you will probably get some resistance, but know that a person's forgiveness should parallel their repentance. If the culprit spouse is serious about keeping the marriage together, he or she will do whatever needs to be done in righteousness to keep the nuptials together. Beware of phrases such as, "We can handle this ourselves," "This should be kept between you and me," or "I don't want anyone knowing my business." These statements should serve as red warning flags!

ATONEMENT

A conjugal breakage must accommodate atonement. Atonement consists of remorse, regret, and regrouping. True remorse is essential in seeking to mend a ruptured relationship. There is a difference between feeling unhappy about getting caught and feeling true remorse for causing what has occurred. A heart that openly acknowledges responsibility for what has occurred is a heart that can more readily be forgiven. The ability to regroup is directly linked to the genuine remorse and regret felt by the culprit.

The atoning effort is a two-sided coin. On one side there is the person seeking forgiveness, while on the other side there is the person who must be willing to forgive. To atone means to make amends. It's an attempt to correct a wrong or transgression. It is essential that the non-guilty spouse knows what he or she wants. Should the relationship go forward or should it be severed? Before the couple can start on the road to recovery, both parties must be fully committed to working on the marriage.

Yes, the innocent spouse as well as the culprit will experience real pain during this process. However, the marriage will never make it off the ground until the non-culpable spouse forgives. Atoning involves making the necessary efforts to amend on behalf of the culprit and the willingness to forgive from the non-culprit. Both are essential to restarting the marriage. When a marriage regroups, it starts all over. Couples get back to becoming sensitive to one another's needs. Courtship is resumed and proper attention and respect are mutual; the little things become the big things that were once missing.

Chapter Two
Who Blew Out the Candle?

Regardless of how long a marriage has been in place, no marriage is an automatic success. Nearly half of the marriages that occur in America end in divorce. Much of this can be attributed to the misnomer about marriage. Just as people marry for different reasons, people differ in their ideology as to what makes matrimony work. All of us are products or by-products of our environment.

Unfortunately, many of the unions we view as being normal are probably abnormal. Abnormality breeds abnormality. As normal as most people are in other areas of their life, when it comes to marriage, I am amazed at just how abnormally they think.

Whether it is our siblings, parents, friends, or someone we hold in high regard that influences us, others play a pivotal role in shaping our ideology. Yet the divorce rate has reached pandemic levels, because all too often, couples do not listen to positive influences, or in other ways do their homework. In many instances, it's only after the marriage has been consummated that they discover their values, ideas, and concepts of both life and marriage are often vastly different.

Just because a marriage has been together for a long time gives no immediate grounds to rejoice. Marriages are often held together because of toleration and time rather than love, trust, and friendship. Most of us would be shocked to learn that many marriages are merely marriages on paper.

Although this chapter is about who blew out the candle, it is important to note that some marriages never had the candle lit. However, that is a topic for another time.

God desires that your marriage thrive and not merely be alive. Nuptials that are built on strong commitment, friendship, and love are marriages that usually have their flame burning bright. Just because a marriage starts off this way doesn't mean it will continue this way. Commitment, trust, communication, and love are all foundational essentials needed to keep matrimony strong. If it seems that all of the aforementioned essentials are present, but your marriage is still suffering, you must pinpoint the problem.

INITIATION MUST
LEAD TO CONTINUATION

In this chapter, we will discuss basic reasons why the flame goes out. One reason the flame goes out on the candle is because initiation does not lead to continuation. The bottom line is someone or both parties in the relationship started something they did not finish. I consider my marriage with my bride of over thirty years to be a great one. However, you can imagine that over the past three decades, we both have grown a lot and have learned a lot. I learned early in my marriage that if you are not capable of continuing what you initiate, it will come back to bite you.

When Maxine and I first married, I would take her and two of her sisters out all the time. It was nothing to pick them up or have them follow us to a restaurant to get a bite to eat. I spared no expense. However, near the end of the second year of marriage, the little money I had was gone. Talk about the last of the big-time spenders. As a matter of fact, Maxine was unaware that I had pulled one over on her, beginning on our very first date.

Several years passed before I would bring myself to tell her that I barely had enough money to pay for our first date. I had $42 to my name and the bill came to $41.89. I still believe today that the waiter is still calling me everything but a child of God. I spent so much time attempting to impress my wife until the "impressive me" outran the "real me." Once the "real me" caught up with the "impressive me," Max realized that my initiation did not lead into continuation.

From the time of courtship until the marriage is consummated, scenarios like this take place in countless relationships. Although I eventually came to my senses and saw the error of my ways, sadly many couples do not rebound, because they remain in the suspended state of impression. We often laugh about the incident today, but things could have ended so differently for us. Unfortunately, there are many relationships that never recover from episodes like ours.

Having said that, it is important to understand that marriages we deem as models are not necessarily what they appear to be. There are scores of couples who mistake growing old together as growing together. Sometimes, the longer the partners in a marriage are together, the more problematic that marriage becomes. Flames blow out because couples fail to keep them lit. A change of pattern is one of the biggest contributors to flame death.

THE WICK AND THE WAX

There are two basic elements responsible for putting

out a flame. These are the wick and the wax. The wick is the string or cord that keeps the flame burning. The larger the wick, the larger the flame will be on the candle. The next time you get the opportunity to examine a candle, you will more than likely notice that the wick is coated with wax. This provides the fuel source when the candle is lit.

As the flame consumes the wick, the wax provides the fuel that brings about the constant consummation of the wick and candle. Both the wick and wax are essential to keeping a candle lit. If you attempt to light wax without a wick, you will never be successful. On the other hand, if you light the wick when it is not enclosed in wax, it will burn extremely quickly.

Courtship often differs from marriage because couples burn the wick that has no candle. Remember, a wick that is not enclosed in wax will burn fast. The wax fuels the flame. Any time a marriage does not have the right balance, it will either burn too fast or it will not burn at all. The part that burns too fast is the wick, which parallels the courtship. The part that will not burn at all is the marriage, which parallels the wax.

Burnout is the result of initiation not transmuting into continuation. A change of pattern is often at the root of a dead flame. A change in perspective usually follows a change of pattern. The latter deals with changing how you do things, while the former deals with how you see things. New jobs, bills, children, illnesses, and stress are just a few factors that are responsible for changing patterns and perspectives.

All of the aforementioned examples bring about certain adjustments in our life. However, if we fail to re-adjust from our adjustment, the marriage that was made in heaven will be a marriage in need of help. It has been said that insanity is to repeat the same behavior but hope for a different result. The flip side of insanity is to change doing what you once did yet expect the same results.

A CHANGE OF
PATTERN AND PERSPECTIVE

A change in pattern is nearly always attributed to a change in perspective. In other words, you no longer view your spouse in the light that you once did. Broken patterns are often the result of broken perspectives. Our perspective is our view of the world or people. Whenever you think differently about someone, you feel differently about them.

Examples of broken patterns and perspectives can range from a couple's finances to their love life. Say, for instance, there was a time in your relationship prior to which, when operating out of your budget, your spouse consulted with you. However, purchases and withdrawals are now being made without your knowledge. In addition, when you now inquire about particular transactions, your spouse becomes defensive. This can be attributed to a change in pattern and perspective.

Although there had once been a time when there was open communication about the finances, there is now hesitation and reservation about discussing them. The same holds true for your love life. If you had a decent or perhaps somewhat vibrant love life and now it can be described as being cold or lukewarm at best, it is a sign that a pattern and perspective have been broken. It is important to understand that whenever your spouse views you in a different way, he or she will begin to treat you differently.

Love or intimacy cannot be turned on or off like a spigot. The $64,000 question is, why do these things occur? They occur because of a lack of carry-over. It amazes me how the courtship is often worlds apart from the marriage. When the value of the courtship is not carried over through the consummation of the marriage, the union is destined for troubled waters.

ANTICIPATION DOES NOT MATERIALIZE INTO REGULATION

The Word of God establishes the premise for marital success. Whenever husbands and wives deviate from the foundational truths of Scripture, they place their marriage in quicksand. Genesis 2:24 asserts, "Therefore a man shall leave his father and his mother and hold fast to his wife, and they shall become one flesh" (ESV). Every marriage involves a degree of anticipation. Scores of marriages fail because anticipation does not materialize into regulation. Newlyweds often demonstrate a different level of affection toward one another than does a couple that has been together for several years.

As a matter of fact, couples whose marriages have grown cold usually find it hard to stomach newlyweds who can't stop touching each other in public. As relationships get busier, both spouses must make a concerted effort to keep a degree of normalcy in their relationship. As mentioned earlier, the wax and the wick play a key role in keeping the candle from becoming a dead flame.

Drafts are another component that can cause the flame to go out, especially the draft of misinformation. Drafts occur when someone leaves a door open. Unfortunately, there are countless marriages that are left to happenstance when it comes to intimacy. Genesis 2:24 places emphasis on three actions: leaving, cleaving, and becoming one flesh. When you fail to fulfill these actions, you will fail in keeping the candle lit in the marriage.

MISINFORMATION

Since all of us are products of what we have experienced or been exposed to, we take our cues from our environment. Regardless of whether a person is saved, most people learned about sex from the gutter. Therefore, in many cases the gutter becomes the reference point for intimacy.

Although the church has improved somewhat in addressing sexual issues, we have yet to bridge the gap in addressing intimate needs in a discreet manner. Therefore, many people go into marriage misinformed. Much of the misinformation about intimacy rests upon personal speculation. When there is a failure to discuss sexual gratification with one's spouse, or to seek competent counseling on the matter, trouble is usually imminent.

When intimate needs are ignored, the relationship usually suffers in some form or another. A strong marriage presents a strong defense against temptation. The more a relationship deteriorates, the more one or both people are motivated to seek intimate gratification elsewhere.

The sex drive is one of the strongest drives known to man. When the Bible speaks of becoming one, it means this in every sense of the word. To place a Ford in a race with a Ferrari is ridiculous. The top speed of a Ferrari reaches nearly 200 mph; the Ford at best can reach 120 mph. Although the Ford is incapable of exceeding 120 mph, both the Ford and Ferrari are capable of doing 60 mph comfortably. The last words in Genesis 2:24 are paramount in understanding the key in keeping the candle lit: *"They shall become one flesh"* (ESV).

The final emphasis in Genesis 2:24 is placed on the word "flesh." The word flesh in Hebrew is *basar*, which connotes body extension. The verse emphasizes that there is not merely oneness in spirit; there is also oneness in flesh. The oneness goes beyond being compatible; it addresses the ability of both parties to be fully vested in the concerns and cares that are critical for marriage.

Understanding the likes, needs, and the desires of your spouse is a part of becoming one. They will not know what you need or desire if you do not tell him or her. On the other hand, if what you need or desire degrades or makes your spouse feel inadequate, you may need to temper your desires. Being one with your spouse is vital to your relationship. Communicating about needs and desires is even more crucial.

Oneness involves being sensitive to the other's personal needs or challenges. The older we get, the more physical challenges we sometimes face. Surgeries, sickness, stress, career changes, children, and a host of other factors can play a pivotal role in altering our sex life. Regardless of what you have seen in the movies or on television, it is imperative that you remain on the same page concerning the intimacy in your relationships.

OUTER TEMPTATIONS

Just as misinformation contributes to a dead flame, outer temptations can have the same affect. Outer temptations usually enter a relationship when sex is being used as a tool. When gratification cannot be found in a marriage, people often begin to look elsewhere. When your spouse for whatever reason neglects you, this can create an emotional void in the neglected spouse.

Drafts play a big part in blowing out candles. Drafts can come as a result of someone quickly blowing past the candle or someone leaving a door or window open. Emotional voids expose the candle of the marriage to the drafts of life.

A failure to participate in resolving intimate differences can lead to isolation. When two people come together to be joined as one, they are to be participators, not spectators or mere commentators. One of the most exciting moments of your marriage should be your wedding night. It should be one of your most exciting moments, not your only exciting moment.

THE LACK OF PARTICIPATION LEADS TO ISOLATION

In his letter to the Corinthian Church, Paul was clear as he laid down intimate responsibilities and requirements for husbands and wives (1 Corinthians 7:3–5). The lack of participation in your intimate life will most definitely cause isolation with either you or your spouse.

Countless marriages have grown cold because of a spouse who has demonstrated introverted behavior. It is not easy for couples to talk about their sexual problems, yet remaining silent will most definitely lead to separation. However, it is wrong to hold your spouse responsible for meeting all of your needs. Your spouse is not responsible for correcting deficiencies in the manner in which you were raised, for your insecurities, proclivities, or self-esteem issues.

Men and women relate to each other from positions that represent two extremes. Intimacy for women is often more emotional than physical. Intimacy for men is more physical than emotional. Failure to understand these differences will make it difficult to overcome the great divide between them. Therefore, communication becomes just as important as physical contact. Failure to attempt to enhance the marriage emotionally and physically will quickly place a strain on the marriage.

When being intimate has become a chore rather than something pleasurable, the marital flame is dead. The result is almost always bitterness, resentment, or blame. Even if the wax and wick are in proper alignment, and the candle is protected from draft, a candle holder is still needed. It is difficult for a candle to burn if it is lying on the ground. The candle holder holds the candle in place so that it may burn to its full potential. When it comes to the intimacy of your marriage, don't be a spectator or a commentator! Participate by holding the candle up.

Chapter Three
Let Me In

One of the biggest dilemmas confronting marriage is caused by hidden hurt. The more the hurt is entrenched, the harder the liberation will be. Unfortunately, there are many people who have suffered at the hands of others; however, they never verbalized their hurt. The nonverbalization of hurt causes one to become reclusive. Living in silence has become the coping mechanism for whatever hurt that has been experienced.

If you were never taught how to address pain, your method of dealing with it may not be correct. People usually act based on their experiences. When pain that has been sheltered, covered, and quieted is released, that release may be uncontrollable.

As I have previously stated, before you can achieve an objective, that objective must first be defined. Exhuming painful memories can be as painful as the actual experience. The longer you neglect to address your hurt, the more that pain is compounded. The journey of a thousand miles begins with the first step. Thus, one of the first steps in allowing your spouse an awareness of your silently borne pain is to pinpoint the behavior that caused it.

Pinpointing the pain means identifying the time, place, person, and other culprits involved in your silent separation. You should know that before any healing can take place, you must deal with the fractures of your life.

Despite the possible success of the coping mechanisms

you used when you were single, chances are these behaviors will not work for you in marriage. If two people are to become as one, it means they must be connected spiritually, physically, and emotionally. To make your spouse privy only to certain parts of your life, but not the most difficult parts of your life, is to leave him or her in the dark. Anytime your spouse feels as though you're holding something back, he or she will feel shortchanged.

Regardless of how healthy or vibrant your marriage is or may seem to have been, when painful memories of the past become present, they will become a constant impediment to your success. If the bumps persist, eventually they will become barricades.

The lack of sharing needful information is responsible for wounding and fracturing many nuptials. No matter how wonderful the person you have married may be, if you fail or become derelict in conveying certain feelings, emotions, and apprehensions, the result will be a loss of confidence in the marriage. Sadly, much of the pain we experienced started during our childhood.

In Matthew 19:19, Christ admonishes us to love our neighbors in the same manner we love ourselves. The interesting thing about this passage is not what it tells us to do, but what it does not tell us to do. Christ said, "We are to love our neighbor as we love ourselves." However, He never tells us to love ourselves. Loving yourself is never discussed in the Scripture because it is automatically assumed that we will love ourselves. Pain is always exacerbated when people do not love themselves. Overcoming the inability to love others must start with becoming able to love ourselves.

It is possible that a person may have a successful job and comfortable life, and still be unable to love himself.

There are untold numbers of well-to-do people who suffer from the insecurity of not knowing who they are. Often these are people who have refused to become involved with someone else because of their insecurities, or perhaps they have taken the opposite approach, seeking date after date after date—but in truth, looking for a match that can never be found.

When individuals stifle their suffering, they risk damaging their self-esteem. Those who are familiar with book bags know that it is a convenient and comfortable way of carrying several books at one time. Unfortunately, the same convenience may apply to dealing with the torment and distress of our past. Mismanaged or mishandled pain often leads one to simply continue carrying the anguish around. There are several potential sources of pain:

- *Emotional neglect* – often occurs when significant others or people you respect fail to show interest in you.
- *Physical abuse* – involves physical harm done to you by family, guardians, or otherwise.
- *Mental suffering* – describes psychological oppression or mental torture.
- *Sexual abuse* – involves sex that is forced upon or used against the will of an individual. It may also involve sexual actions that are illegal or immoral.
- *Child abuse* – can involve one or all of the above.

Stifling can become habitual if proper help is not sought to remedy the pain. Abused people learn to cope with pain by carrying it instead of seeking a cure. These are often people that have a difficult time loving themselves. Because they have successfully carried their pain, perhaps for years, they may become extremely uncomfortable when their spouse makes an attempt to see what's in their bag.

This is a good time to reiterate that if you are suffering in this manner, you may need to seek spiritual or professional counseling. Sharing your past with your spouse is the first step of getting past your hurt. However, the degree of difficulty pertaining to your problem and the length of time that you have carried it may be more than your spouse alone can handle. Therefore, in addition to individual counseling, you may need to be counseled together.

Past experiences help formulate present personalities. We are what we are in part because of what we have been through. Therefore, many marriages suffer because one or both parties experienced an unresolved hurt during childhood. Child abuse often plays a tremendous role in dysfunctional marriages. Child abuse leaves the victim in suspended animation.

When child abuse is not addressed, it can have a devastating effect on a marriage. Emotionally, mentally, and sexually molested people often find it difficult to connect with other people. The aforementioned factors are often kept a secret because of fear, embarrassment, and guilt. It's important for adults to realize that much of what they have experienced as children was not their fault. Children have no advocate or defense mechanisms to deal with hurt. Therefore, they either internalize the pain or act it out through ill behavior.

If you have been victimized, it's time for the "adult you" to address the "adolescent you." People who are culpable of holding things in often make the same mistake in marriage as they do in life. They feel that they can cope with marriage in the same manner they coped with life by merely internalizing crucial issues. In order to address your hurt, you must first communicate with your companion.

COMMUNICATE WITH YOUR COMPANION

A lack of communication often leads to agitation. There are two sources of agitation: the first may come from directly trying to help you, and the second from trying to get you help. Your spouse's inability to help you or get you help may make the relationship extremely difficult. You could very well be in love with a person who is madly in love with you; however, the most wonderful spouse is often agitated when he or she cannot crack the code of your silence. The more you shut your spouse out about your feelings, the deeper a wedge is driven in your relationship.

AGITATION

Despite having a spouse who loves you dearly, closing the communication door will result in your spouse viewing themselves more as a nuisance than a help. The lack of communication brings agitation because it serves as a springboard for mixed feelings. Much of the agitation may come from frequent, albeit well-intentioned, speculation. Questions such as, "What's wrong?," "Was it something I did?," "Are you okay?," or "Let's talk about it" may go unanswered or prompt even greater unrest.

Agitation can often become so severe that the inquiring

spouse tires of asking questions and resolves to merely tolerate the behavior. The more a relationship gravitates toward toleration, the more the relationship resembles a chore. Even good people find it difficult to remain in laborious relationships. There are times in a relationship when circumstances may be totally beyond the control of one spouse; nevertheless, that spouse may feel that he or she failed in preventing the circumstance.

Silent anguish often affects men and women differently, primarily because men are protectors and women are nurturers. For instance, a wife shared with her husband that she was going to the mall. Once at the mall, two thugs assaulted her and stole her purse. Although it was not the fault of either that the assault occurred, the husband often feels a sense of culpability. He feels bad because he failed to protect his wife. Even though there was nothing he could have done, it would be typical for him to insist on bearing part of the blame for not protecting his wife. For her part, the wife may feel an irrational guilt simply for having been victimized.

If the husband suddenly goes into a quiet mode, the wife as nurturer feels a responsibility to crack her husband's code of silence. Much like a mother rescuing a threatened child, a wife will attempt to rescue an aggrieved husband. In summary, when something happens to your spouse, although it may have been well beyond your control, you may still feel partly responsible for not preventing or remedying the occurrence.

ISOLATION

The lack of communicating with your companion is a form of slow isolation. The other day while watching television, I saw a commercial played which addressed certain crimes. The thirty-second clip showed two men who were incarcerated because of their crimes. One offender ate in the prison cafeteria and another played basketball in the prison courtyard. The contrast was watching nonculpable family members who were in prison with the offenders. The offender shown in the cafeteria was accompanied by his mother. She sat eating—and of course she looked extremely out of place. The other offender shot hoops in the courtyard as his young son shot hoops at the opposite end of the court. The moral of the story: when you do time in prison, your family members do the time with you.

Just as awkward as it is to see a mother dressed in her church clothes eating and sipping coffee in a prison café, it is also awkward for a spouse who has been closed out. Your silence and isolation affects them just as much as you would be affected by it—perhaps even more. Remember, they do the time with you. Isolation is a death sentence to a marriage. Life and marriage are about sharing. Who wants to go to dinner only to watch someone else eat?

Communication is serious business. The inability to connect with your spouse produces an enormous rift in a marriage. The lack of communication cannot be ignored. In most cases, it is never the intent of the violated spouse to hurt the nonculpable spouse. Nevertheless, this is exactly what occurs.

VIOLATION

Just as oppressed people often oppress others, violated people often violate those around them. Violations, however unintentional they may be, wreak tremendous havoc on a marriage. The mere fact that something in your past has numbed your ability to communicate fosters multiple violations in regard to your spouse.

Some of the key violations of communication involve trust, competence, and loyalty. Your spouse will feel devalued if he or she is forbidden entry into your silent world. Closing the door on crucial information about your life is a sure way to erode the stability of your relationship. The less access you afford them, the more the trust between you is weakened.

Vows are violated when you marry under false pretenses. Withholding crucial information entering into your nuptials weakens its foundations. To enter into a relationship expecting unconditional love without exposing crucial issues of your past is like building a house on quicksand without a blueprint. In your quest to overcome the demons of the past, you must be willing to commit to a cure.

Committing to a cure means to pursue happiness, not mask pretense. Concealing true feelings leaves them ticking like a time bomb. The more you mask your feelings, the less your spouse is aware of those feelings. The real pursuit of a cure is to obtain triumph and not toleration. Living a life of toleration is living a masked life.

COMMIT TO A CURE

Many settle for toleration rather than triumph because toleration does not entail confrontation. Being committed to a cure means confrontation is a must. Confrontation encompasses tackling the demons of your past. You should know that liberation comes at a high cost. It will take every ounce of faith, guidance, wisdom, energy, and effort you can muster to secure your long-delayed victory. Although in many instances your victory will not be easy, you should know it is attainable.

To truly commit to the cure, you must continue forging forward even when you do not see immediate results. People who attempt to lose weight often become discouraged because they lose inches before they lose pounds. Remember, every step forward is a step out of the wilderness of pain. The journey of a thousand miles begins with one step. Part of seeking a cure involves not penalizing your spouse.

DON'T PENALIZE YOUR SPOUSE

Blaming your spouse or making them the target of your frustration is not committing to a cure. While talking with a former Florida state trooper in my congregation, he shed light on how people deal with pain by assigning false blame. Jeff had been an officer with the Florida Highway Patrol for over twenty years. The last two years with the state, he directed the vehicular homicide division. He was responsible for ensuring that his subordinates complete detail homicide reports in a timely manner. Many of the homicides were the result of DUIs.

After investigating incidents involving vehicular homicide, it was his responsibility to break the grave news to the family of the deceased. On countless occasions of sharing the sad news, Jeff was amazed at how often the grieving family blamed him for the loss of their loved one. He was often hit with a barrage of questions such as "Where were you? You mean to tell me you couldn't stop this from happening?" or "Where is a trooper when you need him?"

Emotional pain is never without blame. However, it's

important to attribute pain to the right place and the right person. While talking to a young pastor who had taken over a struggling church, he told me he had asked, "What can I do to heal the church's hurt?" He had come to the church during a time when the former pastor was at the center of a major rift.

My advice to the young pastor was, be yourself and be careful. I went on to explain pain is never without blame. However, if you spend so much time on the pain, you may well be held responsible for that hurt, despite the fact you were in no way responsible for it.

Although it is not their intent, people often take out their frustration on the nonculpable spouse. Usually this occurs when denial leads to differences. Denied pain manifests itself as deferred pain. Just because the pain has not been expressed doesn't mean it will not be expressed. Unfortunately, when it is expressed, the reaction is often acted out rather than addressed. In many cases when it is acted out, its repercussions are felt by an innocent party. Addressing your pain means you must make a concerted effort to conquer your complex. This requires releasing your faith.

CONQUER YOUR COMPLEX

Roman 10:17 avows, "So then faith comes by hearing and hearing by the word of God." The more God's Word is heard and received, the more faith is increased. The more faith is increased, the more faith can be released. Fear walks down the same corridor that faith walks. The more fear infiltrates your psyche, the less faith you will have. Fear is the assassin of faith. Fear is the Goliath of faith. However, faith is the David of fear.

When you release your faith, you are trusting God to grant you the grace, courage, and strength to confront the complex. The Bible states, "For God hath not given us the spirit of fear; but of power, and of love, and of a sound mind" (2 Timothy 1:7). Romans 8:37 states, "We are more than conquerors through him that loved us."

Conquering your complex parallels the story of David and Goliath. The taunts of Goliath kept Israel in bondage for forty days and nights. Saul's army would have remained suspended in fear had God not sent a ruddy shepherd boy to bring about their deliverance. Astonishingly, the death of Goliath did not come at the hand of Saul or any of his soldiers. To the contrary, Goliath's demise and Israel's deliverance came from an unexpected liberator.

What did David possess that Saul or his army didn't have? The answer is faith and favor. Goliath was a giant that seemed invincible. The more Goliath taunted Israel, the more demoralized they became. Ironically, it was not a sword or a spear that killed the Philistine, but a sling and a stone. The more you delay confronting your complex, the larger it will appear. Why not go forward? The only thing you have to lose is your complex. Amid your fear and faults, put your best foot forward.

WAGE WAR

In conquering your complex, you must make a declaration of war. However, several components must be in place before that war can be waged. No one enters a battle without first calculating the cost. The most basic cost is the carnage. Other factors that must be taken in consideration are strategy and commitment. The strategy involves determining the methodology you will use in subduing the complex. Commitment means enlisting God's help in your war. It is essential to wage war on your complex, because your complex has waged war on you.

Prior to your marriage, you probably learned how to live with your complex rather than conquer it. It is wrong for you to marry and expect your spouse to acquiesce to this behavior. The nature of your complex may include how you feel about your body, intimacy, self-esteem, career, accomplishments, or even your family.

Regardless of what it entails, a strategy must be implemented to conquer the complex. Acknowledging the problem is the first step in the strategy. The second step will be to inform your spouse of your issues, and the third step includes seeking spiritual or professional counseling.

In some cases, there are spouses who possess the ability to help you make it through the difficult times. However, this is a rarity. Although many spouses love their counterparts unconditionally, most will not possess the ability to help you navigate through the troubled waters of your past. The severity of the problem determines the extent of spiritual or professional counseling.

In addition to addressing the strategy, one must address their commitment to the strategy. One of the easiest mistakes to make in attempting to conquer a complex is to take the "half bottle" of antibiotic approach. For those who have succumbed to one infection or another, you are probably familiar with amoxicillin.

Speaking from firsthand experience, I am always tempted not to finish off a bottle of antibiotics. This temptation is driven by the fact that I usually start feeling better before the protocol is complete. Regardless of how soon one begins to feel well, it is important to follow the prescription to the letter.

When you are committed, you will go all the way. Commitment means that if you start the counseling process, you must finish it! Unfortunately, complexes often remain unconquered because a suffering spouse was not committed to taking the full prescription.

Waging war also entails confronting carnage. The severity of your problem determines the severity of the carnage. Addressing the carnage means facing those issues that you have buried, including some that you may never have thought you buried. It addresses the events or incidents you got past, but never got over. Remember, no complex will be conquered until you wage war. Making a decision to fight for your marriage is extremely important, and committing to that decision is of the utmost importance.

BE PATIENT AND SEEK PATIENCE

Once you are committed to wage war, it's important to be patient and seek patience. Rome wasn't built in a day, and in the same sense, overcoming your history of difficulties will take time.

Since we live in such an automated world, we often look for quick and immediate fixes. It is not always the injured spouse who seeks instant relief. Sometimes the biggest problem occurs with the spouse who has had to bear the burden of the complex. In either case, the suffering spouse must be patient and in return seek patience from their spouse.

There definitely will be bumps and bruises on the road

to reclaiming self-esteem and worth. There will be times when you stagnate or experience mild regression. Don't be alarmed, because relapse is often part of recovery.

Chapter Four
Gotta Work at It

The state of Florida offers a discount on marriage licenses for couples who get professional counseling prior to marriage. This gesture is designed to combat the pandemic rate of divorce presently occurring in our state and country. For some reason, there are still many misconceptions that revolve around marriage.

One of those misconceptions is that difficulties and distinctions will automatically work themselves out. This misconception is so prevalent that many couples totally throw caution to the wind. They completely disregard grave indiscretion, gross differences, and gut-wrenching behavior. In doing so, they marry under the pretense that a ceremony or vow will eradicate all their differences.

Much of the alarming divorce rate can be attributed to wishful thinkers. Surprisingly, these wishful thinkers come from various walks of life. However, the professional wishful thinkers surprise me the most. These people are the ultimate professionals when it comes to their career, job performance, and team-building abilities. Their evaluations are above normal. They have promising professional futures because of the skills and talents that make them marketable. One would think that such promise would lead to making good or better choices when it comes to marriage. Often this is quite the contrary.

Somehow, it appears that many professionals take their cue from Hollywood movie stars. Every day we hear about movie stars who marry on a whim. Sadly, this scene is not merely played out in Hollywood, but in literally every neighborhood in America. Wishful thinkers come in all sizes, races, and colors.

SUCCESS IS NOT AUTOMATICALLY TRANSFERABLE

Michael Jordan (MJ) will arguably go down in history as one of the greatest basketball players of all time. Although Kobe Bryant and LeBron James are frequently mentioned in the same breath, in my humble opinion, they cannot hold a candle to MJ. To support my point, here is a list of just some of his many awards and accomplishments:

- Six NBA championships
- Five NBA MVPs
- Fourteen NBA All-Stars
- Six NBA Final MVPs
- One Defensive Player of the Year
- Nine All-Time NBA Defensive First Teams
- Two Slam-Dunk Contest Winners

As gifted as Jordan was in the NBA, his success did not transfer into major-league baseball. After his first retirement from professional basketball, Jordan chose to pursue his lifelong dream of playing baseball. During the 1993–1994 basketball seasons, he took a break and signed with the Birmingham Barons, a Chicago White Sox farm team. As talented as Jordan was on the hardwood, none of it transferred to the baseball diamond. In basketball, Jordan was affectionately called "Air Jordan," but in baseball he was merely known for his name and nothing else.

One is sadly mistaken if they think accomplishments in one area of their life will automatically apply to other areas. Sometimes the greater one's success, the more one is inclined to fail. Success often impairs vision, so we do not see our fallacies and failures. Successful people often feel that their spouse should acquiesce to their wishes, even when those wishes are inappropriate.

Since many accomplished or successful people are accustomed to getting their way, they often anticipate getting their way in marriage. There are times when success and accomplishment can be a two-edged sword. On one hand, they can be a blessing because they afford the niceties of life. On the other hand, they can strangle a somewhat wholesome relationship, especially when they are not balanced.

There was a time in my life when I had become so programmed in my behavior that I attempted to operate my home in the same manner that I operated the church. My bride of over thirty years told me in a quiet but settled way, "Gary, at home your children need their father and I need my husband. We do not need a pastor."

Unfortunately, there are scores of people who are closer to their fame, prestige, success, and accomplishments than they are to their spouse. Many marriages fail because people approach their nuptials in the same manner as they do a business plan. They create business models, charts, and graphs, and in many instances, they fail to understand that the realities of life do not always line up with their theories on paper.

READJUST AFTER THE ADJUSTMENT

Adjustments are a certainty of marriage. The unforeseen

and unexpected are nuptial certainties. One of the biggest dilemmas in a marriage is the failure of one or both spouses to readjust after making adjustments. Parents, friends, and children are just a few people responsible for rearranging our lives. Matters such as finances and careers also play a role in life adjustments. When couples fail to discuss in detail the gravity of their adjustments, it will more than likely put them at odds with each other down the road.

EXAMPLES OF ADJUSTMENTS

Transition from a Two- to a One-Income Family

This can be a blessing and a curse at the same time. The blessing in many instances results in a well-balanced home, especially when children are involved. The benefits of having a one-income family can range from the children eating properly to getting ample help with their homework. However, the difficulty can arise when couples have unrealistic expectations of each other's role.

There are times when the nonoccupational spouse becomes upset because the occupational spouse spends more time at work than they should. Because the nonworking spouse spends more time at home, they sometimes assume that the working spouse also will be able to spend more time at home. On the other hand, the working spouse is under the impression that because the nonworking spouse remains in the home, everything around the house will get done.

Starting a New Job

New jobs will more than likely make demands on a marriage than perhaps were previously experienced.

New jobs or positions are often time-consuming, and come with new obligations, stress, and expectations. New positions and jobs are notorious for infringing upon quality time in a marriage. In many cases, the spouse who has launched into his or her new field or career becomes so consumed with succeeding at their position that they neglect their spouse.

Having Children

Having children takes away from the time you as a couple previously had together. Readjustments must be made due to silent frustration. Most men experience this; however, they feel embarrassed or find it difficult to express.

Newborns demand a lot of time and attention. The care and nurturing they need and are given by their mother build a bond that could not be pulled apart by a team of wild horses. However, there are times when that bond becomes so strong that the connection with her husband seems to be temporarily placed on hold. This adjustment to the newborn means the couple must continually readjust after adjusting to the arrival of the newborn.

Having a Guest in the Home

Allowing someone to live with you causes a major adjustment in the home. Having a guest in the house creates a different atmosphere. Couples often display more discretion when outsiders reside with them as opposed to when they are alone. The guest can sometimes stifle the comfort of the home because of what they need, what they do, or what they lack doing.

Nuptials often become strained, especially when clarity is not established about the guest. Strain can stem from the guest wearing out their welcome, not contributing to the household, or not merely complying with foregone agreements. Agreeing to allow a guest to live with you is one thing, while agreeing on how to get them out is something else. When guests wear out their welcome or fail to be responsible, the spouse to whom the guest is closest often bears the blame.

The longer this issue is not addressed, the more the couple adjusts to a life that is uncomfortable. Regardless of how long the guest stays, the couple must remain on one accord throughout the entire ordeal.

Caring for Loved Ones

One of the biggest adjustments often occurs when we have to care for a family member. The more difficult the issue, the more time and attention it needs. Several years ago, I counseled a member who for five years had given unflagging attention to her father, whose health was failing. For five years she got up at 5:00 a.m. to spend time with her father and did the same in the afternoon after work. Once he died, she and her husband came in for advice on dealing with her loss. After helping her navigate through the range of her emotions, I shared with her that it was time for her to add to her adjustment. During the time of her father's illness, she and her husband adjusted their lives to accommodate her father. Her father's demise meant she needed to readjust to spending more time with her husband.

DEFENDING THE HONOR

Everyone who enlists in the American armed forces signs an oath. Each enlistee must solemnly affirm that he or she will support and defend the Constitution of the United States against all enemies, foreign and domestic. The same holds true for those who unite in the bond of matrimony. You should cherish and honor your spouse. This entails giving each other the utmost support against threats both foreign and domestic. In this context, foreign threats are culprits that have either limited contact or no relation with your immediate household.

Several years ago, while visiting Tampa for a preaching engagement, an encounter led me to defend the honor of my wife. On this trip, I was accompanied by my choir, family, and a few church members. Early that Sunday morning, we all went to the hotel restaurant to eat breakfast. After we had been seated, Maxine and my oldest daughter left for the buffet table while I remained at our table.

Suddenly, a man with another group began to complain loudly to the waiter who served us. The man was angry because the restaurant had not prepared enough food for all of the patrons. Instead of apologizing for the failure to accommodate all of the patrons, the waiter turned to my wife and blamed us for the other group not having enough food. Immediately Maxine told my oldest daughter, "Get your dad!" When my daughter told me what that waiter had said, I flew over to the buffet and let him have it. I also let the cook have it, and the manager, as well as anyone else I thought was involved. Maxine sent for me because she knew I would defend her honor.

Wondering if your spouse will defend your honor and knowing they will defend your honor are two different things. Some spouses may be reluctant to call upon their counterpart because they know their spouse cannot be trusted to defend their honor.

Sometimes it is not a foreign threat a spouse fails to

defend against, but a domestic threat. Domestic threats, in many instances, are more severe than foreign threats. Domestic threats are generally caused by parents, in-laws, and children.

Whenever any of the aforementioned possess more influence in your marriage than your spouse, danger, detriment, and disaster are all imminent. Spouses often become pawns in their own marriage when they truckle to unwarranted family pressure. Unwarranted pressure results when a family member seeks to get you to fulfill their desire even at the expense of offending or transgressing your spouse.

Domestic threats are more difficult to defend against than foreign threats because of closer ties. Children from a previous union often "play the dozens" when it comes to getting their way in a new family. Children are masters at playing the ends against the middle, and making their biological parent choose between them and the stepparent.

Biological children can also be classified as domestic threats. All children know what they can get away with when it comes to their parents. They also know which parent to use to accomplish their task. It is the responsibility of the spouse being lobbied to defend the honor of their spouse.

If your mother or father speaks out against your spouse, it is your responsibility to address that parent. If your child is driving a wedge into your relationship by "playing the dozen," you must take the lead in correcting them. This applies both to biological as well as stepchildren.

The key point is to defend one's honor. Do not misconstrue this with defending dishonor. If your spouse has intentionally placed you in harm's way, there is no honor to defend. It is always easier to defend honor than dishonor. Honor can be defended with integrity; however, dishonor can only be defended with excuses and exaggerations.

DON'T TAKE ME FOR GRANTED

Sometimes the longer you have lived with a person, the more cantankerous one or both of you can become. Part of this occurs because over time, either one of you or perhaps both of you take the other for granted. When a person is taken for granted, it means they are no longer viewed or valued as they once had been. Because time often leads to complacency, the longer a marriage has been together, the harder couples must work at keeping the marriage vibrant.

Countless couples who have been together for years are not happily married. Understand that longevity does not equate with success. Fifteen, twenty, or thirty years of marriage living separately is not what God deems a fulfilling marriage. Therefore, complacency must be avoided like the plague.

Four things to be mindful of so that you do not take your spouse for granted:

1. *It's Ignorant to Ignore*

Ignorance is a major contributor to couples taking each other for granted. When you resolve to hear, yet do not heed warning signs and signals from your spouse, you exacerbate the problem. It is ignorant to ignore issues or concerns that have been voiced by your spouse. Regardless of whether you deem the issues legitimate, if the issues keep arising, they must be addressed, and they must be resolved. Sometimes the longer couples remain together, the more they are prone to ignore each other at times. When this occurs, the marriage is placed upon a slippery slope.

Several years ago, I had lunch with a good friend of mine who was having marital problems. Whenever I would call his home and his wife answered the phone, she would tell me about what he did and didn't do. Although I made mention of her sentiments from time to time, I felt the need to have a face-to-face, heart-to-heart talk with my friend.

As we conversed over our pulled-pork sandwiches, he immediately became defensive. He told me all the things she had done. I suggested that they get counseling and even volunteered myself as a mediator. However, it was all to no avail. About a year later, I received a call from both of them that I will never forget. She called first to tell me that she had moved out of the house. She waited until he went to church and had movers come load certain items. He called later that day to ask if I could do marriage counseling for them. It was too late! It is ignorant to ignore the concerns and issues of your spouse. Regardless of whether they are legitimate, they must be addressed and resolved.

2. *Focus on the Qualities, not the Cracks*

Time has a way of changing us in more ways than one. Unfortunately, instead of relationships automatically getting better, they sometimes seem to automatically get worse. Whenever you begin to take your spouse for granted or vice versa, it means your paradigm has shifted. In other words, you no longer view them in the same manner you once did. This becomes apparent by what it is in which you or your spouse now focus. Focusing on the cracks is focusing on the negative.

Although we all have chinks in our armor, we have qualities as well. Constantly pointing out the negative and never appreciating your spouse's qualities will drive them away from you. Focusing on your spouse's qualities and not their cracks keeps you from getting in a shouting match. Remember, if you live in a glass house, you shouldn't cast stones.

3. *Don't Let Yourself Go*

It is important to continue to take pride in your spouse as well as yourself. Whatever you did to get your spouse, it would be wise of you to keep it up. Marriage is not all based on attraction. However, attraction does play a role in your relationship. People who allow themselves to just let go are people who take their mate for granted. All of us are getting older. The older we get, the more we will be confronted with bags, sags, and bulges. As we age, it's important that we age gradually and gracefully, not quickly.

There are three basic reasons why the retirement age has gone up: limited social program funds, insufficient retirement funds, and greater life expectancy. Many people are living longer due to proper diet and exercise. Prioritizing your health makes you more alert, vibrant, and active. It also plays a pivotal role against disease and sickness. When you eat anything you please and do not exercise, you will more than likely disrupt the quality of life with your mate.

On a recent visit with my primary physician, he gave me some shocking news that blew my mind. He said that 70 percent of the maladies that are presently being treated are preventable. This means 30 percent of the sicknesses people are being treated for are unavoidable. However, this remainder is relatively negligent. Letting yourself go could hasten your spouse to become your caretaker.

Letting yourself go also means forgetting to maintain proper appearances. Sickness and maladies are acceptable reasons for forgetting the importance of appearance. However, laziness and apathy are not. Whatever attracted you to your mate is the same thing that will keep that mate attracted to you. Remember, don't let yourself go!

4. It's a Relationship, not a Routine

Maybe you can remember when your spouse asked you to do something for them and you did it, no questions asked. This was probably because of the quality of your relationship. Unfortunately, over time the routines of life often cause us to throw caution to the wind. We transition from doing things because of our relationship with each other and revert to doing them as if they were routine.

A marriage license, wedding cake, and honeymoon in Tahiti are not chemistry for a thriving relationship. When you stood before the man of God and recited your vows, that was the beginning of your marital journey, not the end.

SEEK TO
BE REASONABLE
RATHER THAN RIGHT

Many people are familiar with the colloquial expression, "You can't teach an old dog new tricks." In other words, once a person gets set in their ways it's hard for them to see, talk, act, or even think differently. Sometimes the longer a couple has been together, the more they seek to be right rather than reasonable. When one or both parties become focused on being right rather than reasonable, this is a problem that must be addressed. It must be addressed because the person seeking to be right will often do it at all costs.

During my car-selling days, the best deals were the ones when I made a little money and the customer received a good deal. When the customer left happy and I made a sale, both of us felt good. This was a win-win deal. A win-win deal afforded me the opportunity to ask my happy customer for referrals. I could ask them to give me a good survey pertaining to how I treated them. Moreover, it afforded me the opportunity to sell the customer another vehicle in the future. All of this was possible because of the win-win deal.

Strained relationships make it difficult for you to ask for grace, especially when you are not accustomed to extending grace. People who portray themselves as being right most of the time usually have very few people that come to their rescue when they fall. People often gloat when you fall because they say you got what was coming to you.

Someone in the service industry has said, "A good customer will bring you three customers, but a disgruntled or unhappy customer will run ten customers away." Can you imagine me asking an angry, belligerent, volatile customer for a referral?

A winner-take-all attitude often creates carnage that makes it difficult to communicate in the future. A winner-take-all person typically wins their battles, but loses the war. They perpetuate a "gotcha" mentality. This attitude can result in your spouse gloating or even rejoicing when you are wrong. All of the aforementioned matters are reasons why you should seek to be reasonable as opposed to being right.

Chapter Five
No Carbon Copies

The Book of Ruth in the Bible is a story centered on a young woman who had an unfeigned love and loyalty for her mother-in-law. This love and loyalty would position her as a vessel in which the lineage of Christ would arise. Her journey began when a Bethlehem family, Elimelech and Naomi and their two sons, traveled to a place called Moab because of a famine in Israel. While in Moab, both sons married Moabite women.

About ten years later, the father and both sons died. After their demise, Naomi departed from Moab and returned to her native Bethlehem. Ruth, Naomi's daughter-in-law, could have remained in Moab, but she made an unusual choice of returning to Bethlehem with her mother-in-law. Once in Bethlehem, Naomi introduced Ruth to Boaz, a relative of Elimelech. Boaz, a well-to-do farmer, showed favor to Ruth because of her piety, love, and loyalty to Naomi and the Lord. He eventually provided for her and married her. It is through this union that David, Israel's greatest king, was born. It is also from this lineage that Christ was born. Although this succinct Book of Ruth unveils a beautiful love story, it is imperative to notice that there are no carbon copies when it comes to marriage. Throughout both the Old and New Testaments, the Scriptures record scores of marriages. Abraham and Sarah, Isaac and Rebekah, David and Bathsheba, Aquila and Priscilla are just a few popular couples of Scripture.

Although time does not allow us to list the countless other couples, you should know that each couple is distinct. The reason for their distinction varies from how they met, lived, persevered, and died.

Since no couple in the Bible is just alike, it is important that you follow the principles of marriage rather than a person in a marriage. Regardless of whether people live up to principles, principles do not cease to be.

IT IS AGAINST THE LAW TO PLAGIARIZE

The word plagiarism comes from the Latin word *plagiary*, which refers to kidnapping. Plagiarism is defined as the presentation of the ideas or words of another as one's own. The academic world views plagiarism as a cardinal sin.

Plagiarism is not limited to academia; marriages too can be plagiarized. Just as no two people are alike, no two marriages are alike. To kidnap (plagiarize) someone else's marriage and attempt to make it your own stifles the originality of your own relationship. It is essential that we revisit Genesis 2:24, because many couples fail to grasp the full essence of this Scripture. The Word of God states that a man shall leave his mother and father, cleave to his wife, and they shall become one flesh. Verse 24 reveals that God said something quite interesting. When speaking to Adam, God said two things to him that do not actually apply to him. Adam is instructed to leave his mother and father and cleave to his wife prior to marriage. What makes the statement unique is that Adam had no mother or father. God spoke these instructions because He was establishing a precedent for humanity.

Every man who joins in the bond of matrimony is to follow the instructions given to Adam. Leaving and cleaving rests upon two premises. Adam's first responsibility was to provide and care for his wife. The second involved his ability to get to know his wife in marriage.

A SECOND GENERATION
IS A COPY OF AN ORIGINAL

A carbon-copy relationship is a relationship void of uniqueness. There is a reason why identical twins in many instances are opposites. Regardless of having been conceived in the same womb, as well as having the same look and having been born at almost the same time, twins may be completely dissimilar in likes, dislikes, and attitudes. Identical twins develop from the same fertilized egg. They are always the same sex and have shared the same placenta, amniotic membrane, and genes.

Despite their similarities, in many instances they are as distinctly different as they are similar. Despite their parents dressing them alike as children, they often grow up with varying tastes. Their differences can apply to tastes in clothes, careers, food, education, and even mates.

There are children who resemble their parents. In addition, there are children who possess similar gestures, mannerisms, and characteristics of their parents. Despite these traits, each is still an offspring of the original. Regardless of how many people tell them how much they resemble their parents, they know they are a second generation. When you emulate someone to the point that you either forget who you are or do not know who you are, you become a phony. Emulation absent of identification amounts to imitation.

One of the worst things you can do is to emulate someone that projects a quality or characteristic they do not possess. Emulating something or someone when you do not have all the facts may lead you to impersonate a perception instead of a reality. Therefore, it is more important to emulate principles rather than people.

THERE IS A DIFFERENCE BETWEEN A REFERENCE AND A COMPARISON

Since I can remember, I have instructed women whose husbands are not saved to use discretion in addressing their unchurched or unsaved husbands. I admonished them to never tell their husbands what their pastor has said. A man does not take it kindly when he is compared to another man. Although this is often not the intent of the majority of the women that I have counseled, the incident occurs quite often. It usually occurs when perceptions are misperceived as realities. Telling him what the pastor said is often translated to "something is wrong with him." The reason men are usually the last ones to call for marriage counseling is it disturbs them to think that another man has to work out their problems for them. Therefore, they often respond by saying things like, "I don't need any man telling me what I need to do," or "The pastor puts his pants on the same way I put mine on." The bottom line is, he is feeling demeaned by comparison.

A man would rather deny or denounce he has a problem before he will confess that he has one. The only time we like personal comparisons is when it either conveniences us or shows us in a positive light. If we are compared to people of nobility, fame, or prestige, this is often a welcomed event.

Usually anything short of that is unacceptable. The same holds true for women. Referencing upholds principles rather than people. Anytime you compare another couple's relationship with yours, you run the risk of treading on thin ice.

MY GOOD TASTE
MAY NOT BE YOUR GOOD TASTE

What tastes good to one person might not taste good to another person. There have been times when Maxine and I have gone to dinner and she has asked me to taste something she ordered. The entrée that Maxine might deem tasty may only seem average to me.

We appeal to others in many different ways. Our appeals often come as the result of the appetites we possess. Appetites in many instances are created by one's history. Whatever you grow in will grow in you. If you grow in passivity, passivity will grow in you. If you grow in low self-esteem, low self-esteem will grow in you. If you grow in patience, patience will grow in you.

History plays a role in determining how a couple comes together and remains together. History is a part of your present and your future. History is something you learn from, turn from, or run from.

Anyone who marries without researching the history of the person they plan on marrying enters a relationship wearing blinders. It is essential to do careful research, because people are not always who they appear to be. History tells a lot about likes and dislikes. History reveals proclivities, personalities, and precepts. Just as people have a history, couples also have a history.

People remain together because of their taste and appetites. Another couple's way of getting along may not parallel the way you would choose to get along. For instance, one couple may get along well because the husband acquiesces to all of his wife's wishes or vice versa. In another example, a husband may cheat on his wife occasionally, but does everything his wife asks of him. A husband and wife can make a good couple while at the same time be awful parents. The bottom line is that there are many factors and variables that determine whether a couple is a model couple.

It is imperative to have essential information about a couple before you admire them. Admiration without information results in mere speculation. In other words, the perception is not the reality. Unfortunately, admiration is often based on limited information. It is only after having the proper knowledge of a person that a proper assessment can be determined. Admiration without accurate information leads to impersonation.

CHEMISTRY IS KEY

Chemistry is the science concerned with the composition, structure, and property of matter, as well as the changes it may undergo during chemical reactions. It is the study of interactions of chemical substances with one another and energy.

Matter refers to the composition of a subject. Matter is anything that has both mass and volume. Chemists have the unique job of studying scores of elements that differ in many ways, including density, acidity, size, and shape. All of these variables determine the composition of matter and their property.

Just because two people are Christians does not mean they will have the same chemistry. A few years ago, while doing spring-cleaning, I tidied up my garage. After moving boxes and discarding things I did not need, I noticed a stain on the garage floor. Noticing the stain led me to wash the garage floor with bleach and laundry detergent. I had used these two cleaning agents before.

When I realized that even the combination was not doing the job, I applied bleach and ammonia. My intent was to take the stain out; however, I almost took myself out! Bleach and ammonia are cleaning agents that cannot be combined because they contain properties that if mixed will release poisonous fumes. The right chemistry really counts!

Matthew 1:18–25 reveals a remarkable story of a couple that had the right chemistry. The passage tells the story of Joseph, Mary, and the Christ child. Although Mary was chosen as the birth mother of Christ because of her virtue and virginity, it is important to know this was not the only reason. There were many other virgins in Israel besides Mary. She was chosen because of the man she was engaged to marry, in addition to her own virtues.

In the ancient Eastern world, if an engaged woman committed infidelity, her intended husband could have her stoned to death. Joseph was determined to sequester Mary in private prior to the angel telling him she had not been unfaithful. Clearly, Joseph was a man of character. The Lord chose to place the baby Jesus in a home that was balanced and temperate. The Lord was aware that Joseph's temperament complemented Mary's and vice versa. Joseph was a man who could listen to his heart, as well as listen to the Lord. A volatile man would have probably had the young, unwed mother stoned to death.

Just because a woman loses her last name does not mean she loses her identity. Marriage is about two people becoming one to create a union. However, even with that union one's individuality is not lost. A good marriage has balance. Balance provides both husband and wife the ability to operate as independently as individuals and in their union homogeneously. Unfortunately, many couples reflect more of a chemical reaction than complement.

THE PRICE THAT
OTHERS PAY MIGHT NOT BE
THE PRICE YOU ARE WILLING TO PAY

The price you are willing to pay will more than likely differ from the price someone else has paid. Someone could have found their "Mr. Right" while they were in their early twenties. However, your "Mr. Right" might not come until you are in your midforties. Sometimes waiting is the price that has to be paid. The price one couple may pay will no doubt vary from what another couple has had to pay, regardless of any price that has been paid.

Paying the price may entail:

- Governing the time of secondary relationships
- Tapering secondary things
- Gravitating more to selflessness than selfishness
- Focusing on living for two, not for one

SOME PEOPLE
SETTLE FOR A MATE
RATHER THAN WAIT FOR ONE

Many people settle down with people that God never

ordained for them. Age, a lack of security or finances, loneliness, sex, and social pressures are just a few reasons why some hastily settle for a mate rather than wait for a mate God has for them. Therefore, the reason some relationships are not all what they are cracked up to be is because their union is unequally yoked.

To hear constant jeering that "you are getting old," "you need to settle down," or "why don't you marry [him or her]?" can drive weak-willed people to the altar. Just because a person is a good man or a good woman is not a good reason to marry them.

Some couples that are considered to be models are nothing more than mannequins. A mannequin is a window dummy. Unfortunately, many couples take their cue from dummy couples.

Several reasons why you should not settle for a mate:

- Don't commit to someone who refuses to totally commit to you.
- Toleration will eventually tire.
- You deserve the best, not the average.
- If you make excuses for them now, you will do it later.

Chapter Six
Guilt Must Never Be the Glue

The state of Florida changed its building and construction codes in the early 2000s due to the devastation caused by several hurricanes in the '90s. It became mandatory that all homes be built to withstand hurricane-force winds. I saw evidence of this change during the construction of my home in 2002.

Before the installers laid and dried the sheet rock, I noticed about every foot within the perimeter of the home, there were steel rods extending from the foundation to the roof. These rods, although inconspicuous, provided an invisible bond that was designed to hold the house together amid a hurricane.

The metal rods were not an afterthought, but were designed in the blueprint of the home. A good builder will never build a home void of blueprints. The drawings are designed to eliminate guesswork.

One reason divorce is so rampant in our country is couples attempt to draw up blueprints after a relationship has commenced. It is difficult, if not impossible, to reinforce a relationship once it has left the station. It can be likened to changing a tire on a car while the vehicle is in motion. Once the relationship gets going and the longer people remain together unrepaired, they often remain together because of guilt.

Guilt-based unions come in all forms, shapes, sizes, and colors. The objective of this chapter is to expose some of the landmines of marriage that are supported by the hangnail of guilt. Although this book primarily addresses ways to mend broken nuptials, this chapter focuses on reasons why people should never marry.

Marriage is a beautiful endeavor when done right. It is also explosive when not done appropriately. Hopefully, you will gain practical insight from this reading that will benefit you and those you love. The list of issues I am about to discuss is by no means exhaustive; however, it should aid you in being aware of a few potential landmines.

MARRY FOR
LOYALTY RATHER THAN LOVE

Never marry someone who is loyal to you but is not in love with you. Guilt becomes the glue when marriage is based on loyalty rather than love. Divorce, most often, becomes imminent when the underpinning or foundational things are replaced with flawed materials. Love, trust, friendship, and communication all serve as institutional essentials. The absence of one of these essentials is a recipe for disaster. Anytime you reduce or barter away the essentials, you reduce marriage to a myth.

Unions that are based on loyalty rather than love are extremely laborious to maintain. Even a good marriage takes work. Marriage that is void of love demands overtime and then some. Those who are loyal to one another, void of being in love with each other, often marry due to convenience.

Despite wanting more, they often settle for less. They have been there for each other, helped each other, and dated on and off. However, age, loneliness, income, and a myriad of other things keep them together. Although the outer shell of their union appears solid, the core consists of guilt-ridden loyalty.

THE OBJECTIVE IS THE OFFSPRING

Even if your life depends on it, never marry because of a child (pun intended). Children top the list in guilt-glued unions. Back in the day, there was something known as a shotgun wedding. Basically, when a young lady got pregnant, the father of the child was forced to do the "right thing" and marry her. If he didn't, the young lady's father would get his shotgun. You can draw your own conclusion from here.

Many good Christian folks acquiesced to this same ideology with a slightly different approach. In times past, the church would often shame men and women into doing the so-called "right thing." Many of these Christians, old-schoolers, and decent people had the right intention, but were wrong. They failed to understand that two wrongs do nothing more than compound a bad decision.

Unfortunately, this has led to children becoming the pawn in a separation. Sadly, prior to the disintegration of the union, the children's lives were already torn apart. Their devastation is often directly related to the ongoing warfare and mind games played by their parents.

Grown-up deceivers produce child deceivers. Adult pacifists create adolescent pacifists. Big enablers engender little enablers. The lives of countless numbers of children are destroyed because they became entangled in the dysfunctional web of their parents' relationship.

Pressuring, forcing, or coercing two people to unite in the bonds of matrimony because they have a child is wrong in every sense of the word. The premise of marriage does not rest upon children; it rests upon love, trust, friendship, communication, and commitment to one another.

When the offspring becomes the objective for marriage, guilt is the glue of the marriage. Entering into a marriage because of children and remaining together only to divorce when the children get older is deception and hypocrisy at its best.

The success of keeping families together is directly related to how the couple initially came together. True nobility is not marrying because you have a child. True nobility is to provide for and spend time with that child you have birthed or fathered.

"I PITY YOU"

You should never marry out of pity. Just as there are those who marry due to the guilt of having children, others marry out of pity. Once again, I cannot underscore the importance of a solid marital foundation. The pressure of marrying on the grounds of kids carries just as much weight as marrying out of pity. Pity occurs when one person loves exponentially more than the other.

The person who lacks the ability to reciprocate affection commensurate with what they receive often marry out of guilt. Why would someone of good conscience do this? It is not done based on one's conscience, but rather emotions. Recipients of love often silently jump through many internal hoops.

They know to a degree that they have taken advantage of their mate's kindness toward them. By not voicing their true feelings about the relationship, their silence leads their mate to sacrifice and invest even more of themselves to the union. This leads to a greater emotional indebtedness.

Therefore, they marry to reward their mate for the sacrifices made, and because they have put up with indiscretions, indecision, and indolent behavior.

This mindset is the perfect recipe for continued indiscretion because marriage is never satisfying to the party that is not in love. When you love someone who at best likes you, you will never be able to fulfill them.

Since there will be a void, more than likely your spouse will search for someone else to fill that void. Being rewarded with the prize of marriage is not a guarantee you will be rewarded with a person who will love you in the marriage.

LEARN TO LOVE

Another relationship held together by guilt glue is the caring but uncommitted relationship. This refers to someone who attempts to learn to love someone that they have not fallen in love with.

Learning to love someone and being in love coexist only on the premise that you fall in love initially in addition to learning to love. There are no substitutes to this concept.

Being in love with a person is defined as the desire to spend the rest of your life with that special someone. This is not a decision based on rash emotions. Being in love involves a convergence of emotions and logic. Ample time must be invested if this is to become evident.

Love at first sight mainly happens in the movies. It takes time to develop true love. It takes time to discover if someone has the same morals and values as you. It takes time to determine someone's goals, religious preferences, political views, hobbies, leisure activities, and even their proclivities. The reason so many people find themselves falling out of love is they fell in love with someone they did not truly know.

When you are in love with someone, you learn and grow to love them. Growing to love someone entails enduring things you would not tolerate. It is done because you're in love. One of the things that ranks at the bottom of the totem pole for me is walking through a mall. I like it about as much as watching paint dry or stomping my little toe.

When Maxine and I visit other cities, I know a visit to the infamous mall is always on the agenda. Over the years, I've become a real champ at this mall thing. Prior to frequenting a mall, I ensure I have certain staples, such as my cell phone and headphones. Once there, I find a coffee shop, a cozy seat, and tell my girl she can browse until she drops.

Time does not permit me to share the myriad of things she endures on my behalf. However, the point is because we are in love, we are willing to learn to love and endure certain things we normally would not tolerate. Attempting to learn to love and endure someone that you are not in love with is like climbing Mt. Everest with shorts and flip-flops. Never marry someone who attempts to learn to love you but is not in love with you.

ABUSE

Abuse before marriage will certainly get worse in the marriage. Emotional abuse is as destructive as physical abuse. Nonetheless, both entail domination, intimidation, and humiliation. Domination involves being treated like an adolescent or as though you are inept. Humiliation is the attempt to assassinate your self-esteem. Intimidation involves bullying you into submission. When a person is programmed to believe that abuse is love, to them, abuse becomes love. This is the reason people leave an abusive relationship only to turn around and enter into another abusive relationship. People who accept abuse as love find it more comfortable and common to remain in unhealthy unions as opposed to wholesome ones. Unfortunately, abuse-guilt has become the glue for many marriages.

ADDICTION

Guilt-addicted relationships are just as strong as the addiction of alcohol, gambling, sex, or pornography (porn). Denial plays a role in nearly every addiction because addictions are built on denial. Let's use pornography as an example. Porn-addicted people often become critical if their spouse cannot keep pace with their sexual desires. They often blame their spouse for a lack of fulfillment.

The insatiable appetite of porn addiction is unrelenting. The super-heightened sex drive has to be supplemented. Pornography is the trick that does the job.

What well-meaning spouses fail to understand is this: all the sex in the world will not stop the porn- or sex-addicted person from wanting more. After being intimate, the porn-addicted mate can go straight to the computer to watch more porn.

The mates of porn-addicted people often run the risk

of losing their identity, scruples, and self-respect. In hopes of curtailing their mate's deviant escapades, they often acquiesce to their sexual wishes. These acts lead them down a road of destruction. Too embarrassed to seek help, the guilt of humiliation keeps them connected to a relationship that they were never truly connected to.

BE HONEST TO YOURSELF

Lying to yourself today will force you to come to terms with the brutal truth of tomorrow. Despite a host of warning signs, people often marry under the illusion that their marriage will evolve regardless of the crises. They convince themselves that their mate will change and they will love away the baggage. Nothing could be further from the truth. These people fail to understand that love doesn't solve problems, solutions do. Albeit, solutions are only useful when like-minded people share like-minded goals and put forth like-minded efforts. This results in the making of a successful union.

Healthy and wholesome relationships are not based on toleration; they are based on trust. In the same manner people research the community where they plan to live, they should do sufficient reconnaissance on the person they intend to live the rest of their life with.

You owe it to yourself to tell yourself the truth, the whole truth, and nothing but the truth.

Face it, most of us have had a relationship that started with a bang and resulted in a bust. When it became evident that the relationship had stalled, you looked for the exit. An exit is better than your destruction.

Marriage from its very inception was designed to enhance life. It is a beautiful thing to witness people who are built for one another become one in matrimony. Marriage does more than bring together a husband and wife. It brings together the couple's friends and family. Sons-in-law and daughters-in-law often feel like sons and daughters to the family they marry into.

Divorce does the opposite. It drives a wedge between family and friends, especially if the divorce is contentious. Here is some final advice. You can do bad all by yourself. Look before you leap. Pray, seek professional or spiritual counsel long before you say "I do" or look for a wedding venue. There is an old adage which states, "An ounce of prevention is worth a pound of cure." Seeking the ounce of advice at the onset will prevent you from needing a pound of cure down the road.

CPSIA information can be obtained
at www.ICGtesting.com
Printed in the USA
LVHW020831021120
670441LV00016B/419